Hertfordshire
COUNTY COUNCIL

Community Information

Please renew/return this item by the last date shown.

So that your telephone call is charged at local rate, please call the numbers as set out below:

	From Area codes 01923 or 0208:	From the rest of Herts:
Renewals:	01923 471373	01438 737373
Enquiries:	01923 471333	01438 737333
Minicom:	01923 471599	01438 737599

L32b

GREAT WESTERN STEAM – south of the Severn

GREAT WESTERN
STEAM
SOUTH OF THE SEVERN

RONALD E. TOOP

D. BRADFORD BARTON LIMITED

Frontispiece The 1.15 p.m. Paddington to Weston-Super-Mare train prepares to leave Bristol (Temple Meads) on the final stage of its journey behind 'Castle' class 4-6-0 No. 5085 *Evesham Abbey.* Alongside, No. 5094 *Tretower Castle,* of the same class, is at the head of a westbound "fitted" freight.   **Opposite** At Bristol (Temple Meads): No. 4967 *Shirenewton Hall* takes over the 'Merchant Venturer' for the last stage of its journey to Weston-Super-Mare. A 'King' class locomotive had worked this train from Paddington.

© copyright D. Bradford Barton Ltd 1973

printed and bound in Great Britain by Mackays of Chatham PLC

for the publishers

D. BRADFORD BARTON LTD · Trethellan House · Truro · Cornwall · England

Introduction

The heart of the old Great Western system began with Brunel's main line from London to Bristol, which linked these two great centres of commerce. Later came the Bristol and Exeter Railway, with a terminus constructed adjacent to Brunel's original terminal buildings at Bristol and from these two stations the present Temple Meads was developed.

At the beginning of the twentieth century, with growing traffic to and from the West of England, the need was felt for a second route from Reading to enable trains to avoid Bristol completely. Three routes which already existed, the "Berks and Hants" line, the Weymouth branch and the single track from Durston were employed, together with the construction of three new cut-off lines totalling 32 miles. This new direct route to Taunton which came into use in 1906 was shorter than the original main line by just over 20 miles. Taunton itself became a bottleneck until the rebuilding of the station and the construction of a flying junction at Cogload enabled up expresses to London via the shorter route to avoid westbound trains from Bristol.

These two principal routes through the area were linked by cross-country services, such as the one from South Wales to Salisbury, which naturally included substantial coal traffic. There were also a number of minor branch lines; one along the Cheddar Valley with its strawberry trade and limestone traffic; the Bristol to Frome branch which helped in the development of the mining industry, two-thirds of the traffic carried being coal; and the former East Somerset line from Wells to Witham.

The territory encompassed by this volume covers the county of Somerset together with part of Wiltshire. It extends from Whiteball and Dulverton in the west through Bristol and Bath to Chippenham and Westbury in the east, an area in which the trains were operated by a wide variety of motive power. Some of the main line sheds from which they operated in the days of steam were Bristol, Bath Road (now a diesel depot), and St. Phillip's Marsh, together with Taunton and Westbury, whilst engine sheds for the branch line services could be found at Minehead, Wells and Frome among others.

After running beside the river Exe in Devon for much of the way, the last part of the journey by an Exe Valley train lay in Somerset. Here, 57XX class 0-6-0PT No. 9685 waits at Dulverton, connecting with a Barnstaple-bound train.

Churchward 2-6-0 No. 6340 arriving at Dulverton with a short train from Barnstaple to Taunt

A scene at Whiteball summit, on the Blackdown Hills which divide the counties of Devon and Somerset: No. 6834 *Dummer Grange* with a Paignton train about to pass No. 5049 *Earl of Plymouth* at the head of an eastbound train for Paddington.

One of the handsome and hard-working 'Castle' class, No. 5092 *Tresco Abbey*, tackles th[e] three mile long ascent to Whiteball summit west of Wellington station.

One of the 74XX class pannier tanks arriving at Ilminster with a Chard-Taunton branch train.

A Taunton to Barnstaple train behind 2-6-0 No. 7326, about to leave Wiveliscombe.
Ahead lies the ascent, including a section of 1 in 58, to Bathealton Tunnel and Venn Cross.

With the wooded North Hill dominating the background, 2-6-2T No. 4143 prepares to leave Minehead with a train destined for Taunton and Paddington.

Taunton to Minehead train arrives at Dunster, the last stop before Minehead, behind
2T No. 6113.

57XX class 0-6-0PT No. 3787 busies itself with shunting in Minehead goods yard prior to heading a pick-up goods along the branch line to Taunton.

2-6-2T No. 6157 marshalling empty coaching stock in Taunton station, 6 April 1962.

No. 1362, of the 1361 class 0-6-0 saddle tanks, introduced on the GWR principally for dock shunting in 1910, waits in the adjacent sidings.

To save platform space in Taunton station, some passenger trains from Yeovil worked right through to Minehead and back; 2-6-2T No. 5548 is here arriving at Taunton with a return Minehead to Yeovil train.

A Taunton to Langport East local behind 2-6-2T No. 4174 approaching Lyng Halt, whic served the two communities of East and West Lyng.

Durston was the junction of the Yeovil branch with the main Bristol to Taunton line; No. 4932 *Hatherton Hall* passes the station with a down "fitted" freight for Plymouth.

At Durston again, in June 1962, No. 5917 *Westminster Hall* on a Penzance-bound express, whilst 2-6-2T No. 5563 waits with a brake van to traverse the Yeovil branch.

'Castle' class No. 4098 *Kidwelly Castle* passing Highbridge with a westbound train in 1961. Note the centrally pivoted signals which were installed in confined locations; also the line to Burnham-on-Sea which crossed the main Bristol to Taunton line here on the level.

A Manchester-bound train leaving Highbridge behind No. 6802 *Bampton Grange.* In the background at right can be seen Highbridge "B" signal box, serving the goods yard on the line to Burnham-on-Sea. This route is being taken [below] by 0-6-0 No. 2204 crossing the Western Region main line.

A Bristol-Taunton train calling at Weston-Super-Mare behind 'Hall' class 4-6-0 No. 6914 *Langton Hall*.

urchward 2-8-0 No. 2875 near Uphill Junction, west of the Mendip Hills, with a west-
und freight train for Plymouth.

Yatton station, situated on a
straight and level section of the
main line between Bristol and
Taunton, was the junction for the
branch to Clevedon as well as the
longer Cheddar Valley line:
0-4-2T No. 1454 on the Clevedon
auto-train (above) and No. 1415
on the Cheddar Valley train
(top right).

In later years the Clevedon service was operated by a two-car diesel set and the Cheddar trains by an Ivatt '2MT' class 2-6-2T. On the main line is No. 4947 *Nanhoran Hall*, with a Bristol to Taunton train.

Journey's end for 0-4-2T No. 1412 with its auto-train, at Clevedon's terminal station, $3\frac{1}{2}$ miles from Yatton.

A pair of 2-6-2 tanks, Nos. 4103 and 6148, head an enthusiasts' excursion train through Congresbury, first station after Yatton along the Cheddar Valley line.

A Cheddar Valley branch line passenger train from Wells to Yatton leaves Cheddar behind 0-6-0PT No. 3795 (top) whilst Collett 0-6-0 No. 2244 departs in the opposite direction (below) with a pick-up goods, after collecting the single line tablet from the signalman.

In 1960 Cheddar station still retained its old Bristol and Exeter atmosphere. The provision of an overall roof was a familiar enough feature of branch line termini, but was unusual at an intermediate station. The wide spacing of the two platforms is a relic of the 7′ 0″ gauge.

ollett 0-6-0 No. 3218 setting off from Glastonbury and Street station with a "mixed" train
r the 12-mile trip to Highbridge along the old Somerset Central Railway.

From Glastonbury, the Somerset Central constructed a 5-mile branch to the cathedral town of Wells where its terminal station was Priory Road. This was closed to passengers in October 1951: 0-6-0PT No. 3795 is seen passing the derelict station with a stopping train from Wells (Tucker Street) to Witham.

The highly successful 'Castles' were developed from the Great Western 'Stars'. In this illustration, one of the latter, No. 4056 *Princess Margaret,* demoted from express work, is departing from Temple Meads with a local stopping train to Taunton in June 1954. She was withdrawn from service at the end of 1957.

he Paddington-bound *Merchant Venturer* rounds the curve into Bristol (Temple Meads)
st Bath Road locomotive shed, behind No. 7034 *Ince Castle,* one of the last of the
astles', built in 1950.

A Collett-rebuilt 4-4-0 of the 9000 class, No. 9008 at Bristol (Bath Road) locomotive shed.

0-6-0PT No. 3759 passing through the original Bristol and Exeter Railway buildings at Temple Meads, on station pilot duties. Alongside is diesel railcar W28W.

A train on the Bristol to Frome branch, at Brislington, a station in the suburbs of Bristol. The locomotive is 0-6-0PT No. 9668.

Pannier tank No. 8746 trundling an assortment of vans and wagons through Bristol's dockland.

Prairie tank No. 5523 sets off from Bristol (Temple Meads) with a passenger train for Portishead: 2-8-2T No. 7250 waits for the road with a westbound freight.

As well as the main line to Paddington, another route from Bristol to Bath was that traversed also by trains from the Midlands and North of England, which left the ex-L.M.S. line at Mangotsfield. In this scene, an enthusiasts' excursion in 1960 is passing Bitton station on this line, behind Churchward 2-6-0 No. 6384.

Bath's ex-L.M.S. terminal station was entitled Green Park at the time of Nationalisatio in 1948. From here, 0-6-0PT No. 3676 is waiting to depart with a train for Bristol via Bitte and Mangotsfield.

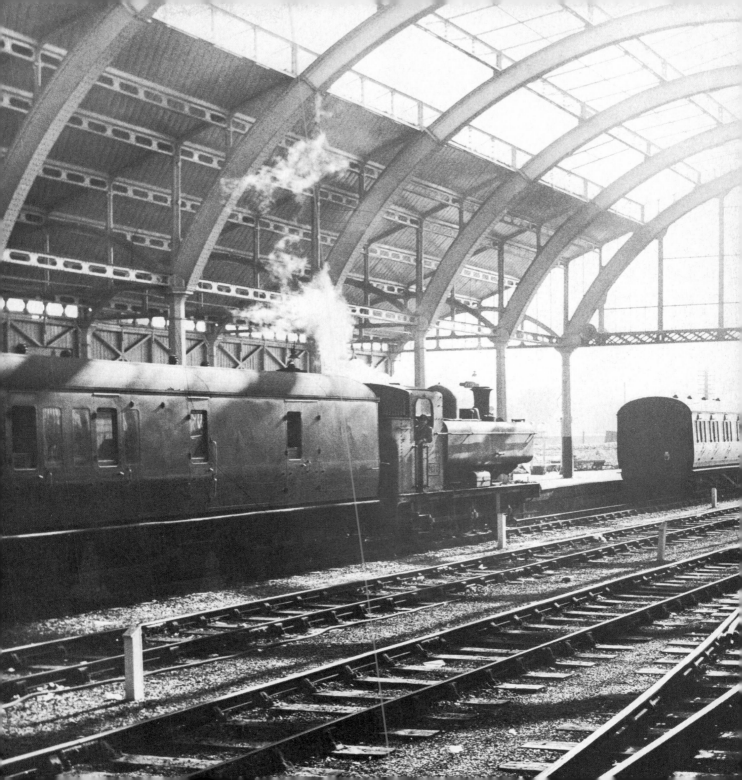

With headboard in position ready to take over the up 'Cornishman' to continue its journey northwards from Bristol, 4-6-0 No. 4083 *Abbotsbury Castle* waits inside Temple Meads.

Hawksworth 4-6-0 No. 1027 *County of Stafford,* built in 1947, arriving at Highbridge with a Bristol-Taunton stopping train.

Highbridge (Somerset Central) station with Collett 0-6-0 No. 2204 arriving with a local train, and another of the same class No. 2219 (left) about to leave with a stopping train for Glastonbury and Templecombe.

Ascending the final mile of 1 in 98 gradient between Castle Cary and Bruton, 'Hall' class 4-6-0 No. 4980 *Wrottesley Hall* with a "fitted" freight for Reading.

On a summer day in 1957 Churchward 2-6-0 No. 5338 ambles along main line west of Bruton with a pick-up goods. Steam still ruled challenged on the Western Region at this date but plans for die isation were in hand.

nother of the Churchward Moguls, No. 5384, draws away from Bruton station with a estbury-Taunton local passenger train.

One of the immortal 'Kings' No. 6026 *King John*, descending the gradient between Bruton and Castle Cary with the twelve coaches of the down 'Cornish Riviera Express'. This was one of the last of the class to receive a double chimney, in 1958.

'Castle' class No. 5032 *Usk Castle* hurries the heavily loaded 'Tor Bay Express' on its w
to Devon past Witham station on a summer Saturday in 1959.

No. 6018 *King Henry VI* at speed past Witham, junction for Wells and the Cheddar Valley
line, with a westbound express for the resorts of Minehead and Ilfracombe.

Trains on the branch line to Wells used a bay adjacent to the up platform at Witham; 0-6-0PT No. 3773 here awaits connections from a Frome-bound train.

Wells (Tucker Street): an 0-6-0PT awaiting departure with the Saturc 11.12 a.m. train from Yatton to Witham.

No. 6935 *Browsholme Hall* with a nine-coach Paddington-Weymouth train takes water from Fairwood troughs between Westbury and Frome.

Running tender first, Churchward 2-6-0 No. 5385, with a train of two auto-coaches, arrives at Dilton Marsh with a Chippenham-Warminster train.

Dilton Marsh is on the 1 in 75 gradient of Upton Scudamore incline out of Westbury; 2-6-0 No. 6374, with banking assistance in the rear, makes a valiant effort on the climb to the summit with a Salisbury-bound mixed freight.

A Birmingham train takes to the lines into Westbury station at Fairwood Junction, behind 4-6-0 No. 4996 *Eden Hall*.

Employed principally for banking on the Upton Scudamore incline, No. 5689, seen at the rear of a freight train near Dilton Marsh, was one of the 0-6-2 tank engines originally designed for service in the Welsh valleys but shedded for service here at Westbury.

With no stop at Westbury, 4-6-0 No. 6834 *Dummer Grange* heads a Paddington train through Fairwood Junction on the by-pass lines.

A doubleheaded Salisbury-Bristol train arrives at Westbury station, with No. 6868 *Penrhos Grange* piloting No. 4973 *Sweeney Hall*. These two classes were maids-of-all-work in the Region for passenger and faster freight trains.

0-6-0PT No. 4604 on Westbury shed (above) and push-pull fitted 0-6-0PT No. 5423 (below) near Bradford Junction with a Warminster to Chippenham local passenger train.

A Frome-bound train, originating from Bristol, leaving Mells Road, last station before Frome, behind 0-6-0PT No. 9668, of the numerous 57XX class, in April 1959.

A coal train from South Wales in the rural depths of the Wiltshire countryside near Bradford-on-Avon, hauled by one of Churchward's 2-8-0 heavy goods. Bound for Salisbury, this had been worked through from Radyr sidings at Cardiff.

Bristol-Salisbury trains; hauled by No. 5978 *Bodinnick Hall* near Bradford-on-Avon and (below) behind No. 6945 *Glasfryn Hall* in the Limpley Stoke valley.

Another heavy coal train from South Wales to Salisbury passing Avoncliff Halt and the bridge carrying the Kennet and Avon Canal, hauled by 2-8-2T No. 7202.

Between Freshford and Limpley Stoke, on the borders of Wiltshire and Somerset, are situated a number of sidings where coal trains from the Cam Valley were marshalled in past days. Here Collett 2-8-0 No. 3834 takes the loop line to permit the passage of a fast train.

A four-coach Westbury to Bristol stopping train leaving Freshford station, behind 'Castle' No. 4084 *Aberystwyth Castle.* This locomotive was withdrawn in 1960, after a thirty-five year life.

0-6-0PT No. 9612 at the head of a pick-up goods train on the Camerton branch line near the junction with the main line at Limpley Stoke.

...lett 2-8-0 No. 3823 heading south along the scenic Limpley Stoke valley with a Salisbury-
...and freight train.

Coal figured prominently in the freight traffic worked over the Bristol-Radstock-Frome line: 0-6-0PT No. 4636 passing Radstock West and (below) a Bristol-bound train passing Hallatrow (for Paulton) station, behind 2-6-2T No. 4131.

Not a passenger in sight as pannier tank No. 4607 leaves the pretty little station at Halla-trow in the pastoral depths of Somerset with a Frome-bound train.

A Frome to Bristol train passing beneath the ex-Somerset and Dorset Joint line between Radstock and Midsomer Norton, on a winter morning in 1959.

▸ther Bristol-bound freight train crossing Pensford Viaduct on the Frome-Radstock-
▸tol line, behind one of the 51XX class 2-6-2 tanks.

A Bristol to Westbury stopping train arriving at Limpley Stoke, behind No. 5942 *Doldowlod Hall.*

Scenes at Chippenham, junction for the 5½-mile branch line to Calne: (top left) a train from Bristol headed by No. 5014 *Goodrich Castle* leaving the station for Swindon; 0-4-2T No. 1446 sets off (below left) with its one-coach auto-train for Calne; (below) Collett 0-6-0 No. 2224 and its freight train arriving at Chippenham goods yard.

No. 5025 *Chirk Castle* passing Mill Lane Halt with the 1.15 pm Paddington to Bristol and Weston-Super-Mare express. Box Tunnel is in the background.

Bristol-Swindon all stations stopping passenger train is seen here drawing away from x and approaching Middle Hill tunnel. The locomotive is No. 7035 *Ogmore Castle*.

A Bristol-Westbury two-coach local leaves the main line to Paddington at Bathampton, behind 0-6-0PT No. 3795.

nother of the 'Castles', No. 5064 *Bishop's Castle,* leaving Bathford Halt between Box and ath, with a Swindon-Bristol train.

A Bristol to Salisbury train commences its run along the Limpley Stoke valley behind one of the many Bristol-allocated 'Halls', No. 6943 *Farnley Hall*.

After a snowfall over Christmas, 'Hall' class No. 5985 *Mostyn Hall*, in immaculate condition after a recent overhaul, accelerates smartly away from Bathampton on the morning of Boxing Day, with a stopping train for Swindon.

Double-chimneyed 'Castle' No. 5057 *Earl Waldegrave,* relegated to freight duties, slogs through Bathampton with a South Wales to Salisbury mixed freight, 19 October 1963.

Spick and span after a spell in Swindon works, No. 6872 *Crawley Grange* passes the junction of the line Westbury and Salisbury, at the head of a Swindon to Bristol train. Bathampton was another confin location where centrally-pivoted signals were employed.

One of the batch of 'Modified Halls' built in post-Nationalisation years, No. 7918 *Rhose Wood Hall*, east of Bath with a short goods train.

Another of the same class, No. 7923 *Speke Hall*, with Hawksworth tender, coasts through the cutting past Sydney Gardens prior to stopping at Bath Spa station, 10 June 1957.

Another of the famous 'Star' class, No. 4053 *Princess Alexandra* leaves Oldfield Park, a suburb of Bath, with a five-coach Swindon-Bristol stopping train. She was built in 1914 and withdrawn in 1954.

he famous 4-4-0 *City of Truro* was removed from the York Railway Museum where it had ent some years prior to 1957 and was then put into service for a time. This historic comotive is seen here waiting to leave Bath Spa with a west-bound train for Plymouth.

The Camerton branch line between Limpley Stoke and Hallatrow, closed to all traffic in 1951, was used in the making of no less than three films. 'The Titfield Thunderbolt' was one of these and the ex-Liverpool and Manchester Railway locomotive *Lion* was repainted to take the title role. 0-4-2T No. 1401, also used in the film, is in the background. Monkton Combe was renamed 'Titfield' for the purposes of film making.

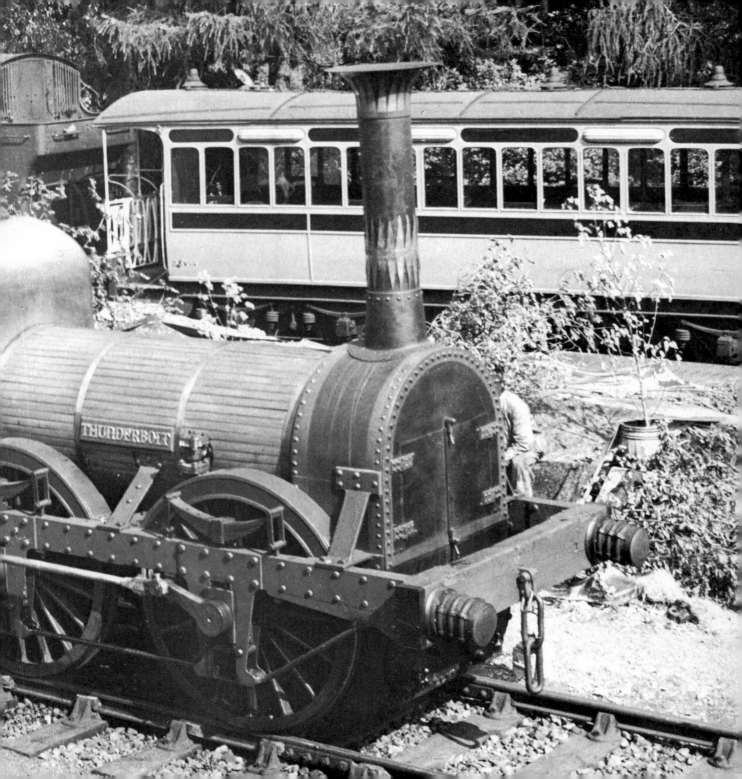

Another 'Modified Hall' No. 6963 *Throwley Hall* at Bath, at the head of an L.C.G.B. tour train.

ollett 0-6-0 No. 2269 emerging from the Twerton unnel with a westbound pick-up goods.

Bristol-Swindon train entering the castellated west ortal of Twerton Tunnel, west of Bath, behind Modified Hall' No. 6969 *Wraysbury Hall*.

One of the efficient little **55XX** class tanks, No. **5564**, makes smart work of a seven-coach Bristol-Swindon train near Twerton Tunnel at the boundary of the City of Bath.

A morning train from Bristol, with No. 4924 *Eydon Hall* at the head, takes
water from Keynsham troughs *en route* for Salisbury.

A 'Stephenson Locomotive Society Special' from Birmingham entering Bristol by way of the old Midland route, and passing Barrow Road shed where all remaining locomotives in the Bristol area were maintained towards the end of the steam era. The locomotives are 0-6-0PT No. 6435 and 4-6-0 No. 7029 *Clun Castle,* the former being on its way to the Dart Valley Railway in Devon—where it is still in operation.

A tranquil scene at Bason Bridge beside the river Brue in central Somerset — Collett 0-6-No. 2204 with a passenger train from Highbridge.

in this series

D. BRADFORD BARTON LTD · PUBLISHERS · TRURO